From the author of
Power of Transparency
An Entrepreneur's Lessons on Balancing it **All**

Navigating the Crisis of 2020

Lisa Liberatore

A publication of:

Transparency Enterprises

Copyright 2020 by Lisa Liberatore
All rights reserved.
Printed in the United States of America
First edition, Softcover
Print : ISBN: 978-0-9989881-3-9
E-book: ISBN: 978-0-9989881-4-6

No part of this publication may be reproduced or transmitted in any form or by any means, electronic or mechanical, including photocopying, recording, or by any information storage or retrieval system, without permission in writing from the publisher.

Workbook design by Edner Mae Fago, E. Mae Media Arts
Back cover photography by Hazelwood Creative

Acknowledgments

This workbook is dedicated to Scott and Dorian. They are my BIGGEST cheerleaders, constantly inspiring me to reach for the stars.

Edner Mae Fago for bringing my vision to life on a page.

Kelly McClymer for her expertise and unwavering support.

Contents

1	Introduction
3	Use Future Success as Your Guide Through Any Crisis
7	Core Operating Principles Still Apply
11	Transparency is a Spectrum
15	Need a Lifeline Here
19	Dollar, Dollar Bills
23	Managing Expectation with Yourself
27	Self-Care is Still Essential
31	Adjusting Habits to Cope with Rapid Change
35	Daily Reflections
39	Celebrate Your Awesomeness
43	Friends Make Life Enjoyable
47	Working with Your Tricky Emotions
51	Managing Expectations with Others
55	Planning for the Unexpected
59	Collaboration in Crisis
63	Flexible Communication
76	Financial Future-Proofing
71	Slow Down and Listen
75	Resources

Introduction

"When we are foolish we want to conquer the world. When we are wise we want to conquer ourselves."

-John Maxwell

This workbook looks deceivingly easy. I keep wanting to fill the pages with more words but the work is not on me. It is on you. I challenge you to think beyond your initial, knee-jerk responses and keep digging to the root of the questions I ask. Your answers will evolve as you evolve. This workbook is not a "one and done." It should be referenced frequently and your own words, ideas and actions are NOT set in stone. They are guiding points along your journey. You can use it for your personal and professional development.

This workbook was inspired by questions I received from people who have read Power of Transparency and wanted to create a plan for themselves and their business in this current crisis. Power of Transparency is based on a personal and professional unexpected crisis that I not only survived but grew tremendously as a result of practicing transparency* with everyone.

Join the Power of Transparency online community to learn how to take the work you do in the workbook and bring those plans to LIFE with support and advice from Lisa and a community of like-minded people. We're here to support you when you feel defeated and cheer you on when you achieve your goals and I'm excited to meet you and help you on your journey. Email me and I'll give you access to the Power of Transparency community.
Email: lisa@poweroftransparency.com

*See Transparency is a Spectrum on page 11 for definition.

Power of Transparency
Navigating the Crisis of 2020 | 2

Use Future Success as Your Guide Through Any Crisis

"The way to get started is to quit talking and begin doing."

- Walt Disney

Knowing what success looks like helps you to stay focused and motivated, even during times of crisis. As of April, 2020, all of my businesses (I have 6+ across various industries) are experiencing economic hardships due to the worldwide crisis we are facing. After the initial shock of the crisis wore off, I was able to shift my focus back to the bigger picture. Envisioning my successful future self. In the initial haze of grieving my new economic reality, I lost sight of the bigger picture. Once I was able to calm down, I realized that my definition of success didn't change but the plan that I had laid out to achieve it did.

What does success look like to you?

_____

_____

_____

_____

_____

_____

How does success impact your current lifestyle? Do you move homes? Do you purchase a vacation home? Do you travel to exotic places?

What roadblocks can you see on the road to success?

What steps do you take to overcome obstacles?

**How will you feel when you are successful?
Hint: You should feel great!**

Create a vision board for what success looks like.

Self discovery is hard work, but you've got this!

Core Operating Principles Still Apply

"When your values are clear to you, making decisions becomes easier."

- Roy E. Disney

While writing Power of Transparency, my mentor urged me to include my core operating principles. I had never stopped to really think about them. My core operating principles came after countless hours of reflection and conversations with those that knew me well. During this time of quarantine, I look at my principles often to keep me focused on who I am. It is easy to become lost when the world around you dramatically changes.

Lisa's Core Operating Principles:
- Take care of yourself
- Trust in a higher power
- Learn to silence your brain
- Think independently
- Just show up
- Do what needs to be done
- Take your job seriously
- If you don't have a solid foundation, you can't expect your business to thrive
- Create a dedicated workspace
- Get organized
- Develop a can do, no fear attitude
- Commit to 'it' daily
- Read
- Make it look easy
- Stay humble

Your list should be unique to you!
What are your core operating principles?

Spend some time thinking. Write it all down but allow yourself to make edits to the list as you mull it over.

Power of Transparency
Navigating the Crisis of 2020

**Your list should be unique to you!
What are your core operating principles?**

Name 10 people that know you well and could assess if your core operating principles are on point.

1. _____
2. _____
3. _____
4. _____
5. _____
6. _____
7. _____
8. _____
9. _____
10. _____

Pause and go for walk.

After creating your core operating principles, reference them in every decision that you make. Whatever question you are faced with answering, go through your principles. If it doesn't align then don't do it. This exercise should simplify your life by providing structure to how you operate.

Transparency is a Spectrum

"Go forward everyday committed to worthy achievement, being altruistic, and building rewarding relationships with the people in your life."

- John Mattone

I believe that transparency is the ability to effectively communicate what is going on with you in that moment. There are different levels of openness but at its core it's being honest with those around you about how you are doing in order to build trust. Transparency allows people to know where you're coming from and gives others reassurance that if I seem uninterested with you that it isn't something they should take personally. It short circuits miscommunication because you are clear on where you are coming from by being able to identify how you are feeling in the moment and not assigning blame. It's not always easy but the reward of doing so is great.

We know those friends on social media that overshare. That is not transparency. That is attention seeking behavior. Know your audience and provide the appropriate amount of information to each. There isn't a formula for saying too much or saying too little. Here is how I process the spectrum of transparency.

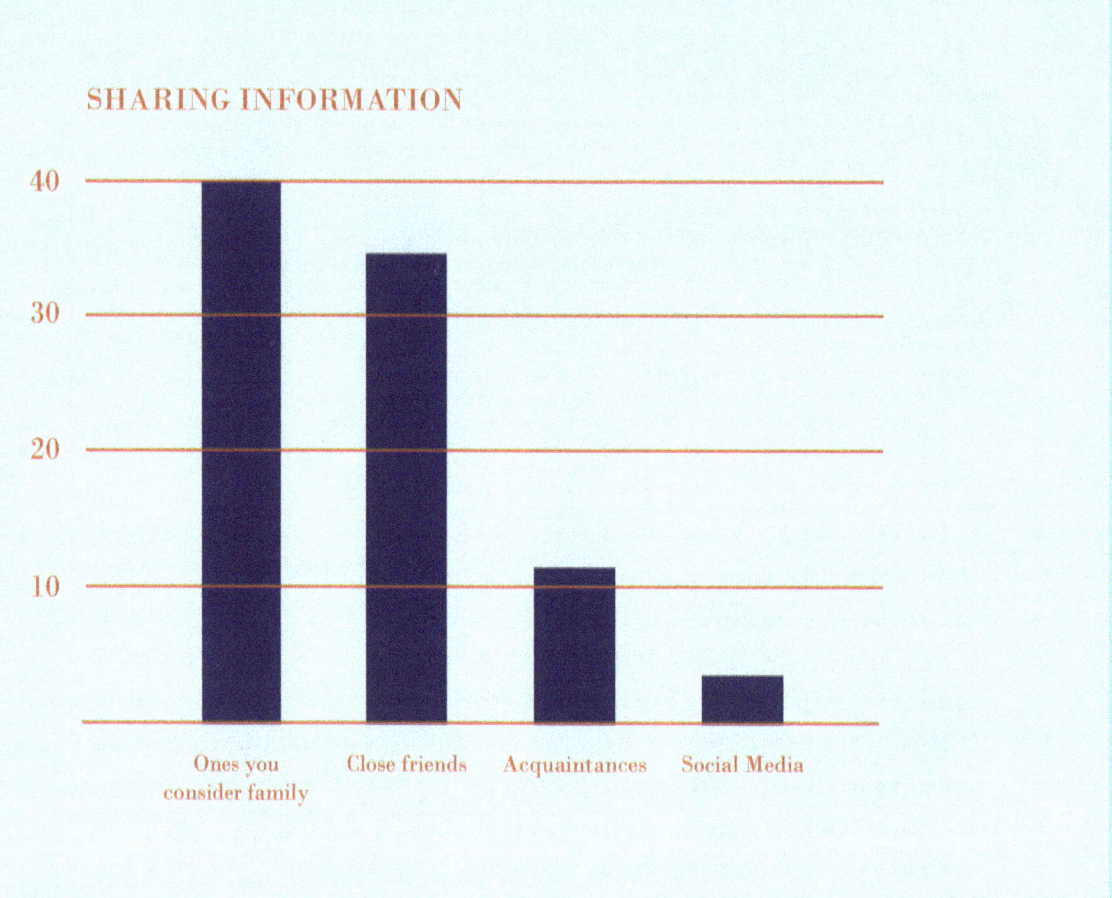

Reflecting on the people in your life, who goes into each of the categories below?

Ones you consider family	Close friends	Acquaintances	Social Media

Draw your spectrum of transparency graph below, then pause to reflect on the results.

SHARING INFORMATION

40
30
20
10

Ones you consider family   Close friends   Acquaintances   Social Media

Note any surprising thoughts or feelings.

Don't forget to drink water!

Power of Transparency
Navigating the Crisis of 2020

Need a Lifeline Here

"Let me remind you that I have a row of electric buttons in my office. All I have to do is press one of them to call the person who can answer any question on any subject I wish to know, relative to the business at hand. I take care of the business, they take care of the questions. Now would you be so good as to explain why, just to answer you questions, I should have a brain stuffed with general culture, when I am surrounded by employees who can supply any information I might want to know?"

-Henry Ford

You should be leveraging other people's expertise to fill in your knowledge gaps. It has become second nature for me to ask for help. I know I am an outlier but promise you can make it your default to ask for help by doing the exercise below. I have found that people want to help and it is OK to not know everything.

When I was getting ready to open my restaurant, I met with a food rep and asked him what he thought I should use for ingredients and to present me a list. He is the expert that has hundreds of customers using various products so could easily create a spreadsheet for me to review that fit my pre-determined criteria. Not only did I save myself a ton of time pouring through thousands upon thousands of products but I leveraged his expertise to make decisions quicker.

What are the *top 10* questions that you are struggling with?

1. _____

2. _____

3. _____

4. _____

5. _____

6. _____

7. _____

8. _____

9. _____

10. _____

Who can help you answer those questions?

1. _____
2. _____
3. _____
4. _____
5. _____
6. _____
7. _____
8. _____
9. _____
10. _____

What's holding you back from reaching out to each person on your list?

1. _____

2. _____

3. _____

4. _____

5. _____

6. _____

7. _____

8. _____

9. _____

10. _____

Reach out and ask for help today!

Dollar, Dollar Bills

"Whatever your income, always live below your means."

- Thomas J. Stanley

Money flows in and out of our accounts daily. It is very easy to just look at the bank account, know you have money and never take the time to critically assess your financial health.
To start:

1. Go over your last month's bank statements and credit cards in painstaking detail.
2. Answer the following questions:
    - Where does your money go every month?
    - Does your current financial picture reflect your ideal financial situation?

From this example, I might want to look a little deeper into my "shelter" bills because that is really taking up a big piece of the pie. Can I downgrade my internet? Do I need to have an energy audit done?

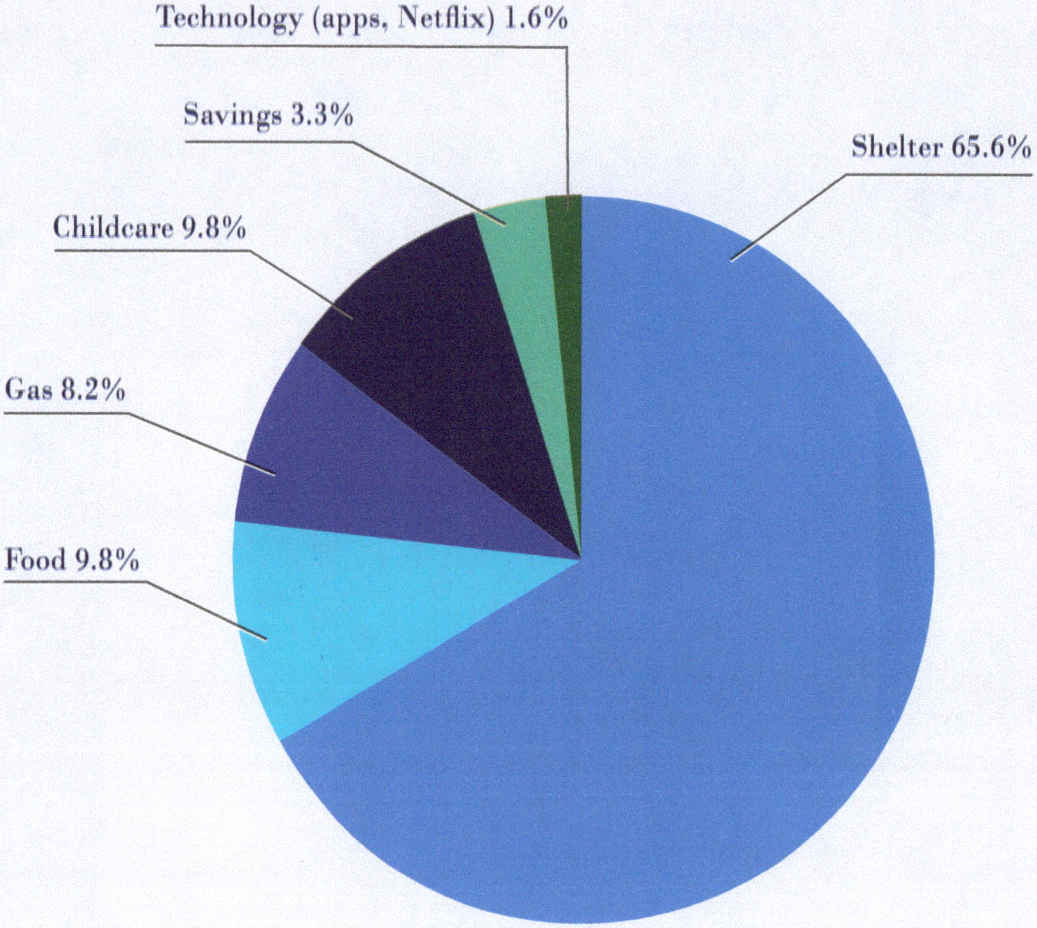

- Shelter 65.6%
- Technology (apps, Netflix) 1.6%
- Savings 3.3%
- Childcare 9.8%
- Gas 8.2%
- Food 9.8%

 Feeling unsure of how to implement this section of the workbook? Join the Power of Transparency Online Community. We're here to support you when you when you have questions and cheering you on when you achieve your goals.

Where does you Money go every month?

Does your current financial picture reflect your ideal financial situation per category?

Category	%
Shelter	
Technology (apps, Netflix)	
Childcare	
Savings	
Gas	
Food	
Credit Cards	

* Add additional categories if needed.

Use this graph to illustrate your current reality.

Use this graph to illustrate how you would like your ideal future financial reality to look.

Breathe! You've got this!

Power of Transparency
Navigating the Crisis of 2020 | 22

Managing Expectations with Yourself

"What screws us up most in life is the picture in our head of how it is supposed to be."

-Anonymous

I don't like clutter and things out of order in my home. My partner does not even notice what I call an "absolute mess." This used to cause me a lot of unnecessary anger and frustration when he didn't immediately spring into action when there was something out of place. I had to accept that if I wanted to have a clutter-free home, then I needed to take lead on it. It isn't a priority for him and I needed to keep my expectations for myself in check, especially during quarantine when emotions and clutter run high!

In order to manage expectations, you first need to know what you need, from whom and for how long?

What do you need?	From whom?	For how long?

 **Don't forget to think about every area!**

Emotionally: To be appreciated
Technically: New computer
Skillset: Better organization

How do you currently compensate for not having the above?
(e.g. I am not and it is a huge challenge.)

What are you intentionally working to improve?
(e.g. reading books, finding a mentor, pricing out new computers, etc.)

Self-Care is Still Essential

"Rest & self-care are so important. When you take time to replenish your spirit, it allows you to serve others from the overflow. You cannot serve from an empty vessel."

- Eleanor Brown

You are the most important person in your business. Are you operating at your highest potential?

Self-care is more important than ever during Covid-19. It is easy to become completely drained living through a crisis. Self-care doesn't have to cost money or take a huge chunk of time. It's about being self-aware enough to know you need to do something because you feel yourself fading. For me, it is as simple as finding peace when it isn't present. It can be through deep breathing, positive self-talk or walking away from work to give my brain and body a chance to re-calibrate.

What does self-care mean to you?

Is self-care part of your daily routine?
Sketch yourself implementing self-care.

What can you do to make sure that self-care isn't something you need to schedule, but is just part of your daily existence?

Be gentle with yourself.

Adjusting Habits to Cope with Rapid Change

"Work like there is someone working twenty-four hours a day to take it all away from you."

- *Mark Cuban*

I have spent years working on good daily habits such as drinking lots of water and eating the daily recommended amount of fruits and veggies. One habit I let slide for years was daily exercise. Slowly, I started developing back problems. It took me several years to finally acknowledge the warning signs that my body had been giving me. I'm proud to say that I've been working out for 6 months. I feel incredible! Habits require DAILY attention. Once the ball gets rolling, it is much harder to stop it.

What warning signs are being presented that you might be missing?

What 5 *habits* are you going to commit to?

1.

2.

3.

4.

5.

Who will hold you accountable?

1.
2.
3.
4.
5.

The key to making a habit stick, in addition to daily attention, is practicing self forgiveness. There will be days when you eat junk food and not a sip of water. Forgive yourself and commit to doing better the next day.

You are STRONG!

Daily Reflections

"Journaling is like whispering to one's self and listening at the same time."

- Mina Murray

Daily journaling was part of my life for over 15 years. It is incredible to open a journal from high school and be teleported back there, re-living the confusing teenager years. With the birth of my son, writing waned but photography took its place. Every day, I capture at least one moment of my life.

However you're capturing your life, DO IT DAILY!

Journal pages just for you. Enjoy!

Write, Draw, Doodle...

Write, Draw, Doodle...

Own your story!

Celebrate Your Awesomeness!

"Celebrate what you have accomplished, but raise the bar a little higher each time you succeed."

- Mia Hamm

One of my proudest parenting moments (to date) is sitting in the front row, watching my 7 year old son being recognized at the Brewer City Council for his leadership in the community by spearheading a fundraiser that raised more than $500 to purchase snacks for kids in need. On a professional level, it was getting this workout created while navigating the transition to quarantining, homeschooling, and all the complexities Covid-19 brought seemingly overnight.

Create a list of all the awesomeness that you have achieved. From professional awards to personal bests like the pecan pie everyone requests at Thanksgiving. Capture those compliments that make you smile and feel proud of yourself.

My *Professional* Awesomeness List

My *Personal* Awesomeness List

What *My Awesomeness* Looks Like

YOU'RE AWESOME!

Power of Transparency
Navigating the Crisis of 2020 | 42

Friends Make Life Enjoyable

"An acquaintance merely enjoys your company, a fair-weather companion flatters when all is well, a true friend has your best interests at heart and the pluck to tell you what you need to hear."

- E.A. Bucchianeri, Brushstrokes of a Gadfly

Genuine friendship is a beautiful thing. Always remember to cherish and cultivate those relationships. A little note arriving in the mail from someone you haven't talked with in months can bring you both so much joy, especially during this crisis when we aren't able to socialize like we used to.

Who are the people you reach out to?

Why are they special to you?

What can you do to improve your friendships?

Reach out to an old friend.

Working With Your Tricky Emotions

"Always remember you are braver than you believe, stronger than you seem, and smarter than you think."

- A.A. Milne

Recognizing and controlling your emotions to create more positive change in your life is an ongoing commitment to being self-aware. As soon as dread creeps in, I've learned to stop and ask why is this feeling rearing its ugly head right now. The answer is usually my confidence in myself and my perceived ability to execute the task at hand. Positive self talk and a call to a friend are my go-to for changing that.

When you feel the following emotions, how do you typically respond?

Anger	Resentment	Fear

Power of Transparency
Navigating the Crisis of 2020 | 48

Stress	Anxiety	Depression

 If you are responding in a destructive way, please reach out for help. There is a list of resources in the back of the workbook. If you don't how you respond to tricky emotions, ask those closest to you, they'll definitely know how you respond.

Draw how you feel right now.

The future is in your control.

Power of Transparency
Navigating the Crisis of 2020 | 50

Managing Expectations With Others

"Great leaders engage in quiet, daily reflection: Did I bring extraordinary value to my family, my team, and my organization? And then make the commitment to bring even more value tomorrow."

-John Mattone

During this pandemic, I am upfront with everyone that I will try my best to meet deadlines and respond in a timely fashion but the truth is, there is no separation between being a mom and a business owner. Now more than ever, we need to manage expectations with others and it starts by checking in with yourself.

Who do you feel you're failing?

1. _____

2. _____

3. _____

Managing Expectations With Others

Have you communicated with that person/s about your feelings? _____
_____
_____

If not, what's holding you back? _____
_____
_____
_____
_____
_____
_____
_____
_____
_____
_____
_____
_____

What steps can you take to change how you feel?

1. _____

2. _____

3. _____

4. _____

5. _____

6. _____

7. _____

8. _____

What will your relationship look like after you express your feelings?

You've got this!

Power of Transparency
Navigating the Crisis of 2020 | 54

Planning For The Unexpected

"Successful people understand that to get results most people don't get, they have to be willing to do what most people aren't willing to do."

- Patrick Edblad

It is uncomfortable thinking about all the "what ifs" in life, but it is important work that needs to be done. Last year, my partner had a life threatening medical emergency that turned me into his 24/7 caregiver for months. Because of the planning my business partners and I had done prior, we were able to minimize the impact to our businesses during that crisis. This section is filled with questions to ponder and to serve as a starting point to create or reinforce systems that need to be in place when the unexpected hits.

Business

▸ Who steps in when you fall ill and can't be at your business for an extended period of time?

▸ Do you have another person listed on your business accounts to be able to handle your finances if you are unable to?

Business

▸ What's your triage plan? Do you have employees that could step into your role? Do you temporarily close? Do you bring on partners?

Personal

Do you have an estate plan? When was the last time it was updated? Does it reflect your current assets and relationships? Do you have the proper insurance coverage so if you can't work, your professional liability kicks in?

Take a break!

Collaboration in a Crisis

"Alone we can do so little; together we can do so much."

- *Helen Keller*

Now is the time to think outside the box! Join the Power of Transparency community for opportunities to collaborate with like-minded people.

When I was first getting Lisa's Legit Burritos off the ground, I had a tiny line item for marketing but I had lots of ideas! Through collaboration with an awesome graphic designer, I was able to barter burritos for marketing materials.

What skills can you trade/barter?

1.

2.

3.

4.

5.

Who could you collaborate with to generate additional cash flow?

1.

2.

3.

4.

5.

Draw what collaboration looks like to you.

Treat yourself!

Power of Transparency
Navigating the Crisis of 2020 | 62

Flexible Communication

"The measure of intelligence is the ability to change."
-Albert Einstein

My preferred method of learning is to be shown a task while also being narrated it but that method isn't for everyone. During the training process with a new hire, I have found that asking them how they learn best is the fastest way to building a positive relationship. If you ask me to read a manual then jump in, I would fail at that job. To be a good leader, you need to be able to flex your communication style to meet theirs.

What is your preferred communication style?

List the communication style for the 10 people you interact most with.	Have you asked them how they prefer to communicate?
1.	
2.	
3.	
4.	
5.	
6.	
7.	
8.	
9.	
10.	

Do you communicate the same way or do you find yourself leaving your meetings confused and not united in vision?

Notes

What are the steps you are taking to adapt your communication style to meet others where they are?

1. _____

2. _____

3. _____

4. _____

5. _____

Breathe!

Financial Future-Proofing

"True success, true happiness lies in freedom and fulfillment."

- Dada Vaswani

My ex-husband and I were business partners in an investment real estate company. As I signed the paperwork to dissolve our business, I realized that this didn't have to be the end of my career as a real estate investor. I needed to focus on financial dreaming and creating a plan to become an investor again. Five years later, I have achieved an investment portfolio 5 times the size of what I had with my ex-husband. Now, I am off to plan my next financial dream. What is your financial dream?

Follow the steps below to help you reach your financial dreams.

What do you aspire to have (e.g. a second home on the ocean)?	What is the price tag associated with those items (e.g. one million dollars)?
1.	
2.	
3.	
4.	
5.	

Power of Transparency
Navigating the Crisis of 2020

Follow the steps below to help you reach your financial dreams.

When do you want them by (e.g. 1 year)?	How are you going to achieve that financial goal (e.g. increase sales by x%)?
1.	
2.	
3.	
4.	
5.	

The future is in your control.
Doodle what it look likes to Dream Bigger?

 *If your financial dream is easily achievable then you are not dreaming big enough!*

The future is in your control.

Power of Transparency
Navigating the Crisis of 2020

Slow Down and Listen

Running a business is a nonstop juggling act with a never ending to-do list. It is easy to get caught up in the day to day routine and lose sight of the vision you had when you opened it. Schedule a monthly check-in with yourself, your business partner and your staff. Make sure it is done in a relaxing setting like a coffee shop. Get their feedback on how it is going and ask for ways to improve business. You might find some new revenue generating ideas while increasing loyalty to your business.

"As soon as I began working at Lisa's Legit Burritos, my very first job, Lisa wanted to learn about my plans for after high school. When I told her I was not exactly sure yet but was leaning toward something to do with businesses, Lisa immediately began thinking of ways to show me as much about the business as possible. She was excited to teach me. That is something I would have never gotten to experience if I had worked at a larger business.

Lisa empowered me during my time working at the shop both in high school and during college. I was then able to relate my first-hand marketing and business management experience to the best business practices I was studying while pursuing my undergraduate degree. Lisa valued my opinion and welcomed my suggestions and ideas. We were always trying new promotions, recipes and ways to get involved in the community. As a small business that was just starting, many things were a learning process for the whole team. Lisa not only helped me get involved with Lisa's Legit Burritos but presented me with opportunities to become involved with Gardiner Main Street and events downtown."

- Courtney, LLB Manager

Notes From Connecting With Your Team

Name: _____

Date: _____

Key take-aways: _____

Notes From Connecting With Your Team

Name: _____

Date: _____

Key take-aways: _____

Notes From Connecting With Your Team

Name: _____

Date: _____

Key take-aways: _____
_____
_____
_____
_____
_____
_____
_____
_____
_____
_____
_____
_____
_____

YOU DID IT!

After meeting with your team, develop a plan to incorporate feedback from your meetings.

Resources

Business

- FAME Relief Loan Program: https://www.famemaine.com
- SBA Disaster Assistance: https://www.sba.gov/funding-programs/disaster-assistance
- CARES Act: https://www.congress.gov/bill/116th-congress/senate-bill/3548/text

Mental Health

- 12 Step Programs
- Alcoholics Anonymous: https://aa.org/
- Narcotics Anonymous: na.org
- Codependents Anonymous: https://coda.org/
- Adult Children of Alcoholics & Addicts: https://adultchildren.org/
- Overeaters Anonymous: https://oa.org/
- Online meetings for all 12 step programs: https://www.intherooms.com/home/category/community-and-meetings/
- Mental Health therapy & coaching: Thebesttherapy.org
- Addiction counseling & coaching: Sobernow.com
- Confidential consultation: Jim LaPierre LCSW, CCS counseling@roadrunner.com (207)-299-4733
- Domestic Violence: (800) 799-SAFE (7233)
- Self Harm: (800) 366-8288
- Suicide: (800) 273-TALK (8255)
- Transgender Suicide: (800) 366-8288
- Grief: (800) 395-5755

 # Power of Transparency Online Community

This workbook is a starting point for changing your life for the better. Join the Power of Transparency online community to learn how to take the work you did in the workbook and bring those plans to LIFE with support and advice from Lisa and a community of like-minded people. We're here to support you when you feel defeated and cheering you on when you achieve your goals. It takes a community for us to unlock our potential and I'm excited to meet you and help you on your journey. Email me and I'll give you a link for the Power of Transparency community: lisa@poweroftransparency.com